The OUTLANDER *Oracle*

A 54-CARD DECK AND GUIDEBOOK

From the world of
Diana Gabaldon

Text by
Valerie Estelle Frankel

Illustrated by
Karina Giada

RANDOM HOUSE WORLDS
NEW YORK

The
OUTLANDER
ORACLE

ike tarot cards, oracle cards act as mediums for personal reflection and inspiration. The symbolism of the cards can guide you to focus your energy and prioritize your desires. While a tarot deck has 78 tarot cards numbered in a prearranged system, oracle cards have no set number of cards and no dictated structure. As a result, oracle cards stand on their own and can be used one at a time to address a question or suggest a path. They can also be read in a multiple-card spread to tell a more complex story.

This 54-card deck is based on the popular *Outlander* books, the phenomenally bestselling novel series with spin-off stories, a television adaptation, and an audience that spans genres, age groups, and interests. The *Outlander* story follows Claire Beauchamp Randall, a married English World War II nurse who steps through a circle of standing stones and is transported to 1743. There, she meets up with a group of Highlanders and falls in love with the brash hero, Jamie Fraser. After many triumphs, tragedies, and a prolonged separation, Jamie and

Claire are reunited for further adventures, including travel to America, where they become embroiled in the Revolutionary War and fight to establish and protect their family and the settlement of Fraser's Ridge.

This deck draws on *Outlander*'s universal themes of love, loss, fate, adventure, conflict, and time to invite fans to access and nourish their true selves and destinies. Twenty-eight cards pull from *Outlander*'s cast of heroes and villains to portray archetypal portraits, like Artificer, Seer, and Seductress. Twenty-six cards explore universal attributes that delve into timeless dynamics and tarot themes, such as Sacrifice, Healing, and Transformation. When used together, the portrait and attribute cards help us meditate on where we have been, discover insight or knowledge to address questions of the day, and intuit a path forward.

READING
THE CARDS

The words on the cards and in this booklet offer sugges-
tions for interpretation. You might approach them with
a specific question or simply an open and curious mind.
Each reader will understand the cards differently, influ-
enced by past experiences, current concerns, and future
hopes. Take note of the emotions that arise as you draw
the cards. Allow your intuition to discern what they may
be telling you.

You can pull one card to help you set a tone or
feeling for the day. A multi-card reading can give
insight into the past, present, and future, allowing you
a transcendent view, like that of the time travelers of
Outlander. Whichever path you choose, take a moment
before you begin and hold the deck. Check in with
yourself. Identify your frame of mind, visualize a
question, or just take a moment to breathe deeply. Once
you have connected with yourself, start your reading.

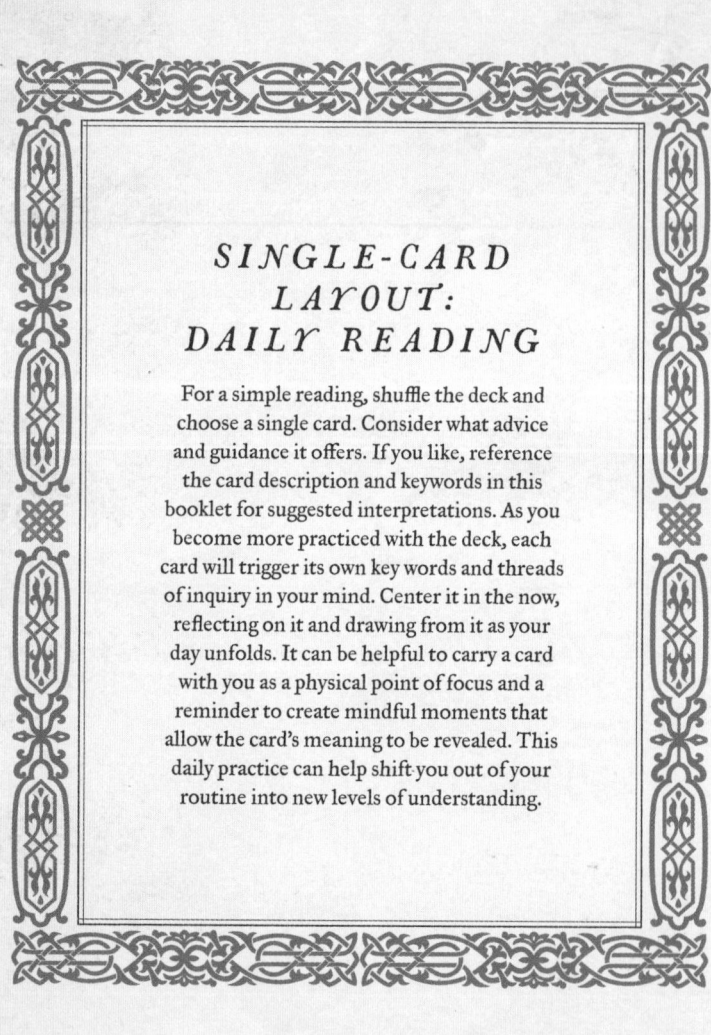

SINGLE-CARD LAYOUT: DAILY READING

For a simple reading, shuffle the deck and choose a single card. Consider what advice and guidance it offers. If you like, reference the card description and keywords in this booklet for suggested interpretations. As you become more practiced with the deck, each card will trigger its own key words and threads of inquiry in your mind. Center it in the now, reflecting on it and drawing from it as your day unfolds. It can be helpful to carry a card with you as a physical point of focus and a reminder to create mindful moments that allow the card's meaning to be revealed. This daily practice can help shift you out of your routine into new levels of understanding.

EXAMPLE 1: CAREGIVER

Sample Interpretation:

Approach yourself and others with a sense of nurturing. As you encounter friends and coworkers throughout your day, be intentional in lending a sympathetic ear and shoulder. Observe how one person might look out for another and offer aid when they stumble. For yourself, try exercising patience and self-control, even in upsetting situations. Diffuse stress by remembering amusing moments, such as when Jenny Fraser Murray nurtured her many children and grandchildren, or by considering how Jenny coped with difficult times. And take a break from nurturing others to practice self-care: Get a special treat or take a moment to start a new project.

EXAMPLE 2: FOOLISHNESS

Sample Interpretation:

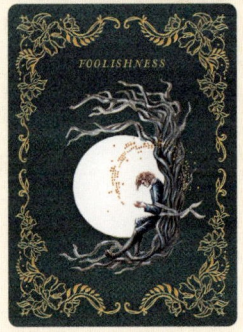

Throughout your day, consider your mistakes and those of others in context, and meet yourself and others with compassion and understanding. Perhaps you/they were trying to accomplish something impressive and noble. Perhaps you/they were trying to show off. Perhaps you/they lacked the training and experience needed for success. Are you about to jump into something new? Let this card speak to you. Is it a warning or a suggestion to pause for a moment to acknowledge the perils involved? Remember that risk can lead to failure and even humiliation, but it can also lead to great reward.

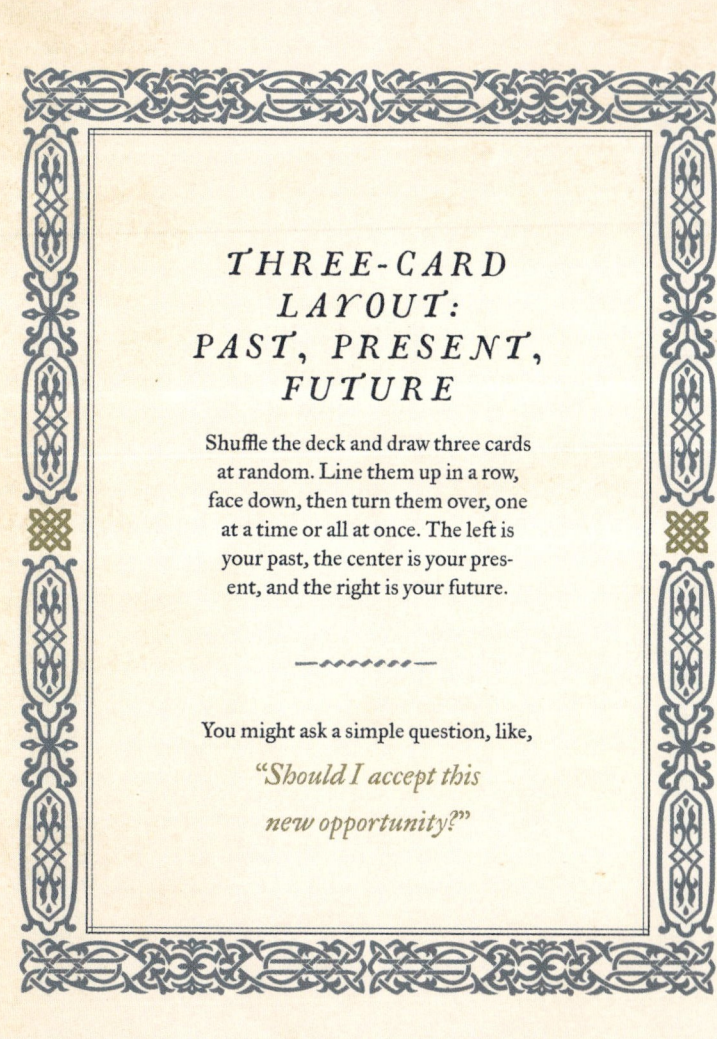

THREE-CARD LAYOUT: PAST, PRESENT, FUTURE

Shuffle the deck and draw three cards at random. Line them up in a row, face down, then turn them over, one at a time or all at once. The left is your past, the center is your present, and the right is your future.

———~~~~~———

You might ask a simple question, like,

"Should I accept this
new opportunity?"

PAST ✦ PRESENT ✦ FUTURE

Sample Interpretation:

This layout could be interpreted many ways: Use the first connection sparked here, or think more deeply. The answers are meant to come from within you. *IMPULSIVENESS* might indicate quick or overhasty decision-making in the past when accepting or rejecting opportunities. The road not taken is always a source of disappointment and longing. On this occasion, it's better to take more time.

LOVERS suggests a current engrossing relationship, not necessarily with a loved one—it might be a passionate hobby or circle of friends. Will taking this job mean following your bliss? Have you been devoting too much time to other pursuits and not enough to career? Or will the new job take too much from what you love?

Finally, the third—Future—card reads *SOLITUDE*. Will the new job be too isolating? Will it be too lonely in a new place? Or will the peaceful solitude bring exactly what you need? Set aside some time now, consider all this imagery and perhaps what the characters chose to do when confronting obstacles in the suggested scenes. With this, you can make a more thoughtful decision.

AS YOU BEGIN

Ideally, you can make these cards your own, choosing what they represent, how they inspire you, and in which ways to apply them to events in your life. Choose the questions that need working through, the ones that have left you stymied. Shuffle through the cards and see how they can point you toward a solution.

As you do readings for yourself and others, follow your intuition. How does each card resonate with you? Think of the characters presented and the moments of their stories and what they meant then and across time as you go about your day, allowing new revelations to come to you. Discuss your interpretations with a friend; you might find a different shade of meaning. Carry a card in your pocket, share a photo spread on social media, or try scrapbooking and journaling on a theme of the day. Reread your favorite *Outlander* moments for further inspiration (or just for fun) and consider what guidance the characters can offer. Enjoy getting to know your cards and listening to what the deck is telling you.

ARTIFICER

INGENUITY

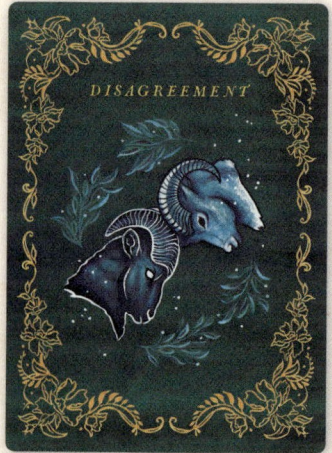

DISAGREEMENT

WANDERER

Portraits

ARBITER

COLUM MACKENZIE

- *Reckoning*
- *Justice*
- *Accountability*

A shrewd authority, Laird Colum MacKenzie makes swift, definitive judgments: His word is harsh but final.

ARTIFICER

BRIANNA MACKENZIE

- *Invention*
- *Innovation*
- *Skill*

Starting something new is a venture that requires a great deal of determination—it all begins with a single spark of inspiration.

CAREGIVER

JENNY FRASER MURRAY

- *Family*
- *Nurturing*
- *Loyalty*

For the parent, patience and self-control are infinite virtues. Jenny Fraser Murray always has a handkerchief and a comforting hand, though she's also a mother bear defending her family.

DEFENDER

MURTAGH FITZGIBBONS FRASER

- *Loyalty*
- *Protection*
- *Caretaker*

Whatever Jamie needs, from guarding his loved ones to keeping the secret of time travel, his faithful lifelong ally, Murtagh, provides.

DISCIPLE

MALVA CHRISTIE

- *Apprentice*
- *Follower*
- *Attendant*

An eager young student, the Disciple is new to her field, absorbing experience and knowledge. Tom Christie's mistreated daughter, Malva, enthusiastically commits to Claire's mentorship and teachings.

FALSE MESSIAH

BONNIE PRINCE CHARLIE

- *Misguided*
- *Disaster*
- *Upheaval*

Charming but overconfident, the prince raises funds across Europe and leads a loyal army of Highlanders to tragic slaughter.

FRIEND

LORD JOHN GREY

- *Fealty*
- *Support*
- *Protection*

A loyal Friend can be relied upon to act with honor, which sometimes must be balanced between patriotism and affection, as Lord John comes to learn.

HANGED MAN

ROGER MACKENZIE

- *Indecision*
- *Perspective*
- *Uncertainty*

Traditionally, the Hanged Man indicates a crossroads: Something the hero desires is at stake, yet it will involve great sacrifice. Roger is repeatedly faced with crossroads, and his chosen paths have led to new experiences and new life.

HERO

JAMES FRASER

- *Brave*
- *Steadfast*
- *Reliable*

The Hero willingly risks his life for those he loves and makes great sacrifices out of courage and devotion. As Claire observes, Jamie proves himself such a champion over and over.

LOVERS

JAMIE AND CLAIRE

- *Soulmate*
- *Eternity*
- *Harmony*

The Lovers indicate a strong, devoted relationship, one for which a person would cross the world or the centuries.

MANIPULATOR

GOVERNOR WILLIAM TRYON

- *Emotional Blackmail*
- *Dishonesty*
- *Deception*

Governor Tryon enlists Jamie to settle Fraser's Ridge, though as a Catholic, Jamie could have his lands revoked at any time. Tryon uses people, and that makes him dangerous.

MENTOR

REVEREND WAKEFIELD

- *Experience*
- *Guidance*
- *Champion*

A trustworthy Mentor is essential on one's journey: generally not a parent but someone who offers love and endless support, like Roger's adoptive father, the Reverend.

MISOGYNIST

TOM CHRISTIE

- *Tyranny*
- *Oppression*
- *Intolerance*

Jamie's fellow prisoner from Ardsmuir, Tom Christie shows a constant disdain for women. His brazen, domineering attitude is reflected in his callous, occasionally brutal treatment of his daughter, Malva.

NARCISSIST

LAOGHAIRE MACKENZIE

- *Selfish*
- *Shallow*
- *Mercenary*

A jealous Laoghaire betrays Claire, shoots Jamie, and demands funds so generous she lives like a queen. Behaving as if no one matters but herself, she becomes a frustrating antagonist.

OUTCAST

YI TIEN CHO

- *Rejection*
- *Withdrawal*
- *Inner Strength*

Forced to flee his homeland forever, Yi Tien Cho makes a life for himself in Scotland and the Caribbean but continues mourning his loss.

REBEL

JAMES FRASER

- *Provocation*
- *Freedom*
- *Authenticity*

The Rebel is true of heart and brave in action, rising up to resist, fight, and speak out for their cause, as Jamie does in the Jacobite Rising and again in the American Revolution.

RULER

KING LOUIS

- *Unethical*
- *Materialistic*
- *Control*

A Ruler with supreme wealth and authority, King Louis of France often values material comforts and regal pride over justice.

SADIST

BLACK JACK RANDALL

- *Danger*
- *Dishonesty*
- *Aggression*

A Sadist tortures and harms others for his own enjoyment. Black Jack Randall represents the worst of humanity, abusing his power to inflict cruelty.

SAGE

CLAIRE FRASER

- *Focus*
- *Contemplation*
- *Inner Guidance*

With age comes discernment, judgment, and experience–even magic, as Claire finds when she reaches full maturity.

SEDUCTRESS

GEILLIS DUNCAN

- *Enticing*
- *Charming*
- *Cunning*

Creative, passionate, and passionately creative, Geillis stretches the boundaries of what is possible through beguilement.

SEER

NAYAWENNE

- *Clarity*
- *Insight*
- *Inner Life*

The Seer or high priestess embodies secret knowledge. Claire's mentor, Nayawenne, helps others see through deceit and grasp the wisdom of the universe.

SPY

FRANK RANDALL

- *Duality*
- *Deception*
- *Control*

Frank spends the war guarding classified reports and undertaking black projects. This foreshadows his keeping of so many secrets in his married life afterward.

TRAITOR

THE DUKE OF SANDRINGHAM

- *Betrayal*
- *Suspicion*
- *Duplicity*

The Duke of Sandringham plays both sides, leaving it wholly unclear whom he truly supports—even his niece falls victim to his scheming.

TRICKSTER

STEPHEN BONNET

- *Deceit*
- *Danger*
- *Untrustworthy*

The Trickster is a figure of transformation in others, upending the status quo and forcing confrontation, as Stephen Bonnet does in his appearances.

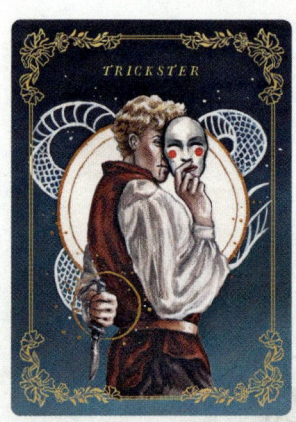

TWINS

JOSIAH AND KEZIAH BEARDSLEY

- *Connection*
- *Strong Relationships*
- *Partnership*

The orphaned and indentured Beardsley twins, Jamie's tenants at Fraser's Ridge, learned to fend for themselves when young, combining their strengths and skills. Two together are stronger than one. In Jo and Kezzie Beardsley's case, two together *are* one.

WANDERER

YOUNG IAN MURRAY

- *Courage*
- *Leap of Faith*
- *Journey*

A perpetual seeker and a lighthearted entertainer, Young Ian Murray is a source of youthful adventure. Those who allow themselves to explore off the beaten path find new experiences, self-awareness, and perspective.

WARRIOR

DOUGAL MACKENZIE

- *Sacrifice*
- *Support*
- *Protection*

A strong man who defaults to fighting and physical conflict, often without considering consequences, Dougal MacKenzie acts as his brother Colum's sword.

YOUTH

JEM AND MANDY MACKENZIE

- *Enthusiasm*
- *Energy*
- *Hope*

Young people like Jem and Mandy represent raw talent, plans that have not yet solidified, and an unjaded, uncynical optimism.

Attributes

ABYSS

Jamie after the Battle of Culloden.

- *Heartbreak*
- *Loss*
- *Resilience*

Out of darkness comes light. After the Battle of Culloden, Jamie lies in a heap of dead men, gravely wounded and ready to die, while his beloved (and pregnant) Claire is in another time. Yet he is spared and, somehow, finds the will to live.

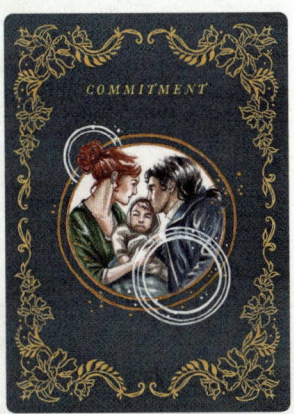

COMMITMENT

Roger commits to Brianna and their baby.

- *Evolution*
- *Courage*
- *Self-Discovery*

Marking their baby with his blood, Roger commits to abandoning the future and staying in the past with his new family.

CONFLICT

Jamie and Dougal fight.

- *Chaos*
- *Turbulence*
- *Opposing Forces*

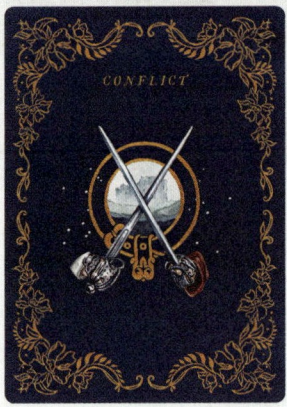

When facing opposition, you must stand your ground and defend your position. Know that when you use force or intimidation in personal conflicts, you risk losing the respect and cooperation of others.

CREATION

Claire pulls from her experience, knowledge of herbs, and available tools to improvise and innovate.

- *Promise*
- *Beginnings*
- *Inspiration*

An artist approaches a project with dedication and, with will, shapes a work of the heart. This brings positive energy, a productive mindset, and a sense of achievement.

DECISION

Claire at Craigh na Dun.

- *Intuition*
- *Empowerment*
- *Action*

There are two options: to stay or to go. Claire weighs the pros and cons of her choices.

DISAGREEMENT

Hal and Dottie argue.

- *Conflict*
- *Misalignment*
- *Clash of Ideas*

Strong-minded individuals with differing perspectives are often at odds with each other, as Hal, the Duke of Pardloe, and his rebellious daughter, Dorothea, find.

FOOLISHNESS

Sixteen-year-old Lord John tied to tree.

- *Careless*
- *Untamed*
- *Naïve*

Taking risks can lead to great
success, but for young Lord John,
it could also result in defeat and
humiliation.

HEALING

Claire's oath to do no harm.

- *Repair*
- *Care*
- *Mental and Physical Health*

From tending to WWII soldiers as
a nurse to building her knowledge
of botany to care for the wounded in
the 1700s to becoming a doctor and
surgeon in the 1960s and growing
into her mystical powers, Claire's
lifework is to heal.

HELPLESSNESS

Geillis and Claire tied up in a pit.

- *Lack of Control*
- *Fear*
- *Inner Critic*

Outspoken Geillis and Claire are trapped and could be burned as witches if the local judges condemn them. The two feel trapped and without choices, but with ingenuity, a new answer can present itself.

HOME

Lallybroch.

- *Peace*
- *Security*
- *Belonging*

Lallybroch, in the Scottish Highlands, is a constant center and source of stability, heritage, and self for the heroes, even as they create new homes.

IMPULSIVENESS

Young Fergus Fraser rides an unbroken horse.

- *Spirited*
- *Immature*
- *Lacking Wisdom*

Feisty and quick to quarrel, young Fergus has the potential to be a hero but has yet to learn the restraint of maturity.

INDUSTRY

Jenny spins at home.

- *Focus*
- *Vision*
- *Diligence*

Jenny Fraser Murray exemplifies everything expected from a lady estate holder: practicality, perseverance, good management, and education.

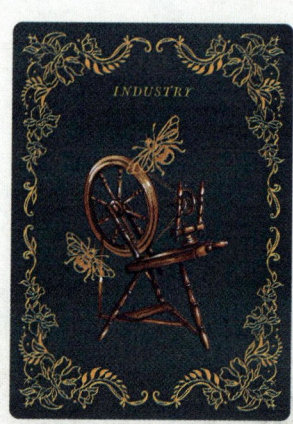

INGENUITY

Jamie and his men before the Battle of Prestonpans.

- *Resourcefulness*
- *Willpower*
- *Inner Strength*

When outnumbered, like Jamie and his men against the English, one learns to find a solution through stealth rather than direct conflict.

JOURNEY

Lord John on a ship.

- *Adventure*
- *Change*
- *Lessons*

The water element signifies a need to walk away from ordinary life and search for something more, as is the case when the *Porpoise* carries Lord John to the Caribbean.

JUDGMENT

Claire judges Master Raymond and the
Comte St. Germain.

- *Justice*
- *Accountability*
- *Values*

Judgment represents trial and
consequences, leading to transition
and rebirth. It emphasizes the
importance of clear decision-making.

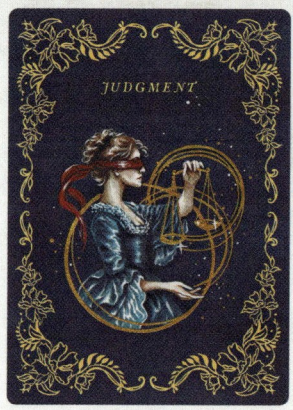

KNOWLEDGE

Denzell Hunter studying.

- *Higher Learning*
- *Power*
- *Healing*

Dr. Denzell Hunter, like Claire,
assiduously seeks wisdom and uses it
to help others.

MARRIAGE

Marsali marries Fergus on their tropical island.

- *Bond*
- *Partnership*
- *Union*

Marriage represents a union of opposites, a coming together of balance and love, as Marsali and Fergus find on Hispaniola.

PATIENCE

Frank waits for Claire.

- *Space*
- *Stillness*
- *Adjustment*

Frank must resign himself to Claire's disappearance and await her return, and then wait longer for their marriage to heal.

RISK

Jamie scales the walls of Fort William to rescue Claire with an unloaded pistol.

- *Courage*
- *Unknown*
- *Wings*

Jamie often leaps forth, taking risks and acting on instinct, as he does when he rescues Claire from Black Jack at Fort William.

SACRIFICE

Old Ian Murray.

- *Martyr*
- *Offering*
- *Dedication*

An impulsive hero, Ian Murray is quite fearless and tenacious, though this has resulted in a terrible injury. The wounded soldier was a man of great courage, now left to remember past glories.

SATISFACTION

Building Fraser's Ridge.

- *Fulfillment*
- *Well-Being*
- *Achievement*

Hope, energy, and hard work combine to deliver the contentment and gratification of accomplishing an important task, as when Jamie and Claire build and rebuild the Big House on the Ridge.

SOLITUDE

William Ransom fishes at Mount Josiah.

- *Retreat*
- *Contemplation*
- *Isolation*

The Hero must wait to reflect and grow spiritually before acting. William Ransom, the illegitimate son of Jamie Fraser, takes time to think at his refuge of Mount Josiah after discovering the secrets of his birth.

SPIRITUALITY

Rachel sits under the stars.

- *Meditation*
- *Openness*
- *Beacon*

Seeking spirituality means letting go
of the self and seeking wisdom from
a higher power, as Rachel Hunter
does often in accordance with her
Quaker beliefs.

THE TOWER

*The burning of the Big House at Fraser's
Ridge.*

- *Upheaval*
- *Chaos*
- *Change*

Change can be traumatic and
heartbreaking, as it is for Claire and
Jamie when their precious home at
Fraser's Ridge burns to the ground,
but it can also bring renewal and
revival and a strength in rebuilding.

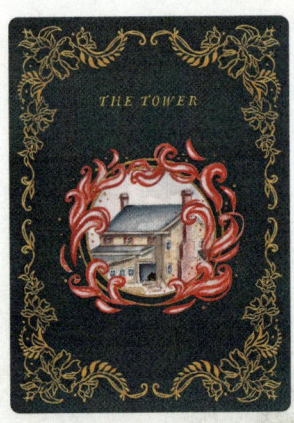

TRANSFORMATION

Master Raymond in his apothecary shop.

- *Awakening*
- *Becoming*
- *Creativity*

The apothecary or magician is the mystical creator and changer of the world to suit his liking. Master Raymond can read auras and help patients harness their center to heal. He also brings transformative potions, charms, and knowledge.

WEALTH

Jacobite gold.

- *Abundance*
- *Increase*
- *Fortune*

Some of the missing French gold sent to aid Bonnie Prince Charlie during the Jacobite Rebellion resurfaces at River Run, apparently cursing those who come to it with impure intentions. Wealth may find you in a cave, in the Scottish Highlands, or simply in a turn of luck.

DIANA GABALDON is the #1 *New York Times* bestselling author of the wildly popular *Outlander* novels—*Outlander, Dragonfly in Amber, Voyager, Drums of Autumn, The Fiery Cross, A Breath of Snow and Ashes* (for which she won a Quill Award and the Corine International Book Prize), *An Echo in the Bone, Written in My Own Heart's Blood,* and *Go Tell the Bees That I Am Gone*—as well as the related Lord John Grey books *Lord John and the Private Matter, Lord John and the Brotherhood of the Blade, Lord John and the Hand of Devils,* and *The Scottish Prisoner;* a collection of novellas, *Seven Stones to Stand or Fall;* three works of nonfiction, *I Give You My Body . . . , The Outlandish Companion,* and *The Outlandish Companion, Volume Two;* the *Outlander* graphic novel *The Exile;* and *The Official Outlander Coloring Book.* She lives in Scottsdale, Arizona, with her husband.

VALERIE ESTELLE FRANKEL is the author of 100 books on top franchises, from Star Wars to *Outlander*. She lives in the San Francisco Bay Area.

KARINA GIADA is an American watercolor artist currently based in Taiwan. She focuses primarily on watercolor portraits and has worked with a number of authors, designer brands, and publishers.

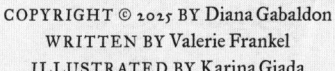

Published in the United States by Random House Worlds, an imprint of
Random House, a division of Penguin Random House LLC, New York.
RANDOM HOUSE is a registered trademark, and RANDOM HOUSE WORLDS and
colophon are trademarks of Penguin Random House LLC.

ISBN 978-0-593-58139-1

Printed in China

EDITORS: Sarah Malarkey and Jacinta O'Halloran
DESIGNERS: Jessie Kaye and Laura Palese
ART DIRECTOR: Jenny Davis
PRODUCTION EDITOR: Kelly Chian
EDITORIAL ASSISTANT: Lydia Estrada
PRODUCTION MANAGER: Maggie Hart
COPY EDITOR: Kathy Lord
PROOFREADERS: Anna Carson, Uthman Adejumo, and Megha Jain

First Edition

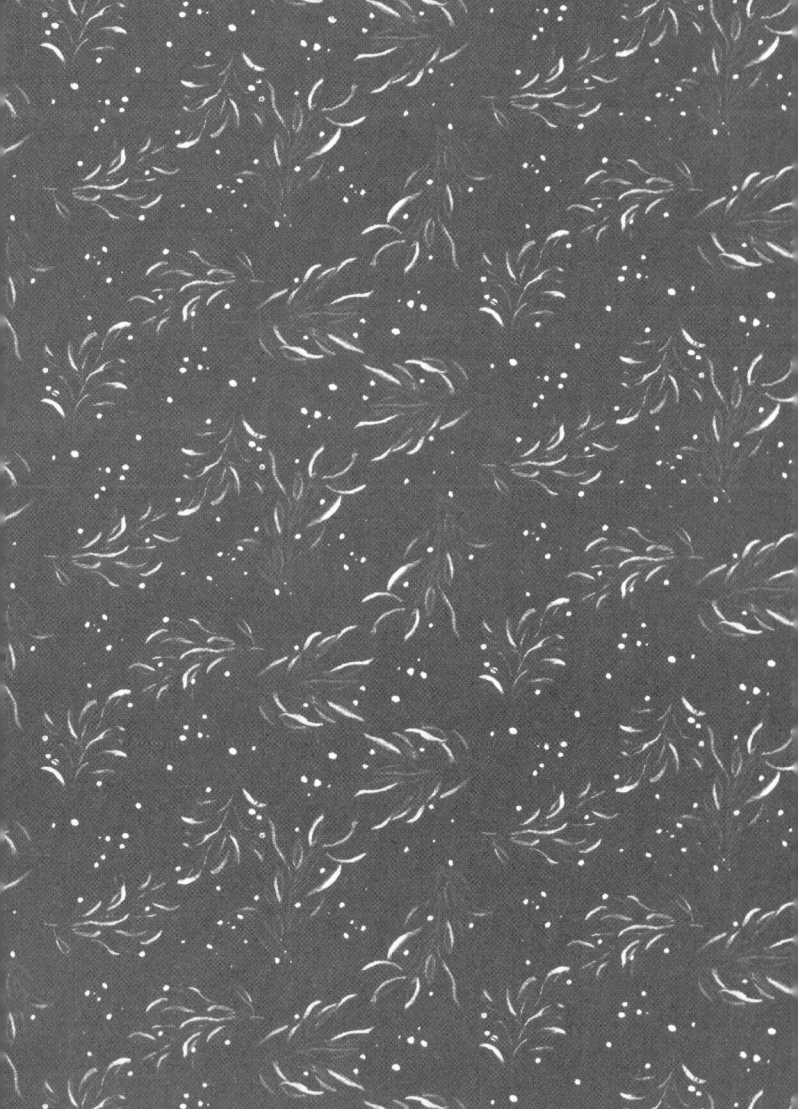